Dealing With Waste

WASTEWATER

Sally Morgan

Smart Apple Media

This book has been published in cooperation with Franklin Watts.

Editor: Rachel Minay, Designer: Brenda Cole, Picture research: Morgan Interactive Ltd., Consultant: Graham Williams

Picture credits:
The publishers would like to thank the following for reproducing these photographs:
Corbis 22 (Ted Streshinsky); Ecoscene front cover main image (Rosemary Greenwood), 6 (Pat Groves), 7 (Angela Hampton), 8 (Matthew Bolton), 9 (Barry Hughes), 10 (Alan Towse), 11 (Robert Nichol), 12 (Vicki Coombs), 14 (Michael Cuthbert), 15 (Edward Bent), 16 (Barry Hughes), 17 (Tom Ennis), 18 (Jon Bower), 19, 20 (Wayne Lawler), 21, 23 (Chinch Gryniewicz), 24 (Melanie Peters), 25 (Sally Morgan), 26 (Paul Thompson), 27 (Tony Page); i-stockphoto front cover top right (Stephen Gibson), front cover bottom right (Micha Fleuren).

Published in the United States by Smart Apple Media
2140 Howard Drive West, North Mankato, Minnesota 56003

Library of Congress Cataloging-in-Publication Data

Morgan, Sally.
Wastewater / by Sally Morgan.
p. cm. — (Dealing with waste)
Includes index.
ISBN-13: 978-1-59920-013-2
1. Water—Purification—Biological treatment. 2. Sewage—Purification—Biological treatment.
I. Title.

TD475.M67 2007
363.72'84—dc22   2006035136

9 8 7 6 5 4 3 2 1

Contents

Using water

Water is essential for life. About 97 percent of the world's water is salty and cannot be used for drinking. Of the rest, 2 percent is frozen in the ice caps and in glaciers. This means that just 1 percent of all the water on the planet is suitable for drinking and other uses.

This river in China is being used for washing. Just one toilet flush in the developed world uses as much water as the average person in the developing world uses for a whole day's washing, cleaning, cooking, and drinking.

Everyday uses

People use water every day for cooking, washing, cleaning, and heating. Water is also used to water gardens and clean cars. Industries use large quantities in manufacturing processes, and farmers use it for their animals and crops. All of these everyday uses create lots of wastewater.

Think about the different ways that you use water each day. How would you cope if you had to collect your water from a tap in the street?

The average American uses about 89 gallons (340 l) of water a day. That's much more than people living in other parts of the world. A European uses about 53 gallons (200 l). Someone living in the dry parts of Africa, such as the Sudan, uses just 4 gallons (15 l).

More people use more water

As the number of people in the world increases, so does the amount of water that is used. Many people do not think about the water they use. Every time they turn on a tap, water pours out. However, in many of the hotter parts of the world, this is not the case. There are shortages and even droughts when rain does not fall for months or sometimes years.

In this book, you will read about the different ways that wastewater can be treated and learn about ways in which everybody can help reduce the amount of water that is used.

Watering a garden using a hose uses far more water than a watering can, and some water ends up on sidewalks or paths rather than on the soil.

Wastewater

Wastewater has to be treated or disposed of carefully so that it does not pollute, or harm, the environment.

Types of wastewater

There are different types of wastewater. Water that has been used for washing or cleaning contains soaps and detergents. Water that has been used to flush the toilet is called sewage, and it contains urine, feces, and toilet paper, as well as harmful bacteria. Wastewater that has been used in industry may contain chemicals. Water that runs off farmland in wet weather may contain fertilizers and pesticides.

This river in El Salvador is polluted with sewage and garbage. Few animals could survive in the water.

Water pollution

In the past, wastewater was simply emptied into rivers and oceans, and this caused water pollution. For example, huge piles of foam from detergents were seen floating on the surface of rivers. Today, this sight is less common because modern detergents are biodegradable and break down in the water. Also, less untreated water is put into rivers and oceans. However, in many developing countries, untreated sewage and other dirty water is emptied straight into rivers and oceans. This kills fish and small animals that live in water.

Sewage has been emptied into the water through this pipe, and it has killed all the fish in the water.

It's my world!

How clean is your local river or lake? The next time you walk past it, look at the water. Can you see any garbage floating in the water? Occasionally, factories or farms have accidental spills of chemicals. If you see a number of dead fish floating in the water, contact the local water authority and let them know.

Street water

As well as wastewater from sewage, there is urban runoff. This is water that flows down streets and into storm drains during wet weather. The water picks up garbage and chemicals from the street such as oil, paint, and pesticides. During heavy rains, the wastewater in the sewers may overflow and mix with rainwater in the storm drains. Unfortunately, this wastewater usually empties straight into rivers or oceans.

Treating sewage

Clean drinking water comes into homes through one set of pipes and leaves as wastewater through another set, called sewer pipes. This wastewater has to be treated.

Clearing the waste

All of the wastewater produced by a city eventually ends up in a river, lake, or ocean. On its way, this wastewater flows through a sewage treatment plant. The sewage treatment plant treats the sewage so that the wastewater is clean enough to be emptied into a river or ocean. The treatment plant separates the solids in the sewage from the liquid part. Then the liquid part is cleaned using living organisms.

Clean water from a sewage treatment plant in Florida is emptied into a marshy area.

Fungi are important decomposers because they break down dead and decaying matter and return nutrients to the soil.

Natural breakdown

In natural habitats, animal droppings are broken down by fungi and bacteria. This process is called decomposition, and fungi and bacteria are called decomposers. The products of this decomposition are nutrients, which can be used by plants. The decomposers recycle the nutrients so that they can be used again.

Sewage treatment plants rely on natural processes to break down the sewage, copying the natural process of decomposition. Sewage contains a range of waste materials, so different microorganisms are used to make sure all of the waste is broken down. The products of decomposition are harmless to the environment, and the water is clean.

Sewage treatment plants

The treatment of sewage in a sewage treatment plant is divided into three stages.

Pretreatments and primary treatments

Pretreatment is the removal of large objects that may be mixed with the sewage. The sewage is chopped up and emptied into large settling tanks. In the primary treatment stage the solids are allowed to sink to the bottom of the tanks. Only about two-thirds settle. The rest remain floating in the water.

Modern sewage treatment plants can be quite large. Here, the primary treatment takes place in the large tanks at the front. Beyond are the beds where the secondary treatment occurs.

Treating the sludge

The solid mass at the bottom of the tank is called sewage sludge. Composting is a good way to recycle it. The sludge is moved to an enclosed tank containing microorganisms where it is gently heated to about 104 °F (40 °C).

This is the ideal temperature for the microorganisms that feed on it. Once the sludge has been broken down, it is cooled and the microorganisms die. The sludge is now safe to handle and can be used as a compost.

How Sewage Treatment works

Raw sewage

↓

Pretreatment
1. Screening to remove large objects
2. Grit removal

↓

Primary treatment
Sewage into settling tanks → Sludge removed

↓   ↓

Secondary treatment
Filter beds to remove small particles → Composted

↓

Water into final tanks to
allow tiny particles to settle → Water to be used as drinking
water is chlorinated and piped to houses

↓

Clean water into river or sea

Secondary treatment

The next stage is to remove the remaining solids from the water. The water is either trickled over a filter bed or piped into large tanks where air is bubbled through it. In both cases, microorganisms feed on the bacteria and solids in the water.

The water may look cloudy after this stage because there are still lots of tiny particles floating in it. To remove these particles, the water is passed into another tank and left for a few days so the tiny particles have time to sink to the bottom. If the water is to be used as drinking water, is has to be treated with chlorine, a chemical that kills any bacteria in the water. (This is similar to the chemical that is used to treat water in swimming pools.)

It's my world!

See if you can find out where the sewage from your house goes. Many sewage treatment plants arrange tours for members of the public so that they can learn more about the sewage treatment process.

Reed beds

In many parts of the world there are no sewers to carry away sewage. It has to be treated where it is produced. An environmentally friendly way of treating sewage is to use plants called reeds.

It's my world!

Reeds grow in the shallow water around lakes and in marshy areas. They are tall plants, up to 6.5 feet (2 m) high, with long grass-like leaves. They grow close together, forming dense clumps. Next time you are in a park with a lake or in the countryside, look for reeds at the water's edge.

The wastewater from this hotel in Scotland is piped into a reed bed. Then the clean water is emptied into this large pond.

Why use reeds?

Reeds are plants that are found in wetland areas, and they thrive in shallow water. Unlike most other plants, reeds can take in oxygen from the air through their leaves and transport it to their roots. There, the oxygen bubbles from the roots into the mud. The oxygen in the mud encourages the growth of lots of useful microorganisms.

Separating out the solids

The sewage is usually collected in large underground tanks. The solids settle to the bottom of the tank. The solids build up as more sewage is added, so they have to be removed every so often. The wastewater is then piped into reed beds.

Water hyacinth is a fast-growing floating plant. In many countries, it is a problem because it clogs up rivers, but now in East Africa it is being used to clean up wastewater. Afterward, the plants can be composted.

Cleaning the water

The reed beds are large, shallow containers, lined with concrete and filled with reeds. Wastewater is allowed to trickle through the mass of roots, where it comes into contact with millions of microorganisms. The microorganisms feed on the tiny particles in the water. Clean water drains out the other end of the reed bed.

Large-scale systems

Reed beds are not just used for treating wastewater from homes. Large-scale reed bed systems are now being built to treat the waste from visitor centers in national parks and from isolated hotels and villages. Reed bed systems have also been built to treat the wastewater from industrial sites, farms, and fish farms.

Desert sun and fishponds

Sewage treatment plants are expensive to build, and they require a lot of maintenance. Many of the developing countries of the world cannot afford to build lots of sewage treatment plants, so sewage is treated in a different way.

Using heat

In some desert areas where the climate is hot and sunny all year, the solids are separated out, then the wastewater is pumped onto the ground, where it evaporates in the heat. Any bacteria in the water is killed by the heat of the sun.

The water evaporates to form a vapor that rises into the sky and forms clouds. It falls back to the ground as rain.

Did you know . . .

Green composting toilets are often used in remote places. They do not use any water. The toilets are simply buckets or containers with a seat. After each use, some sawdust is sprinkled over the waste. Once the container of waste is full, it is emptied onto a compost heap. The compost heap is carefully managed so that temperatures in the middle rise high enough to kill all the harmful bacteria.

The hot desert temperatures evaporate water from this pool of sewage. In time, microorganisms in the water will break down the waste, and the water will evaporate.

Harvesting fish

Fishermen from Kolkata, India have developed a sewage treatment system that is cheap to run, environmentally friendly, and provides jobs for thousands of people. It treats about one-third of the city's wastewater. Solids in the sewage are separated out, and the water is taken by canal to large, shallow ponds. The wastewater warms up in the ponds.

There is plenty of light, so plants in the ponds grow quickly. The ponds are used to breed a type of fish called carp. The carp feed on the plants. More than 16,500 tons (15,000 t) of carp are caught each year and sold to local people. Although the carp live in water from sewage, they are safe to eat. This is because the plants help clean the water, and microorganisms eat any harmful bacteria.

These people in Israel are harvesting fish that have been bred in wastewater.

Managing the ponds

The system has to be carefully managed. December and January are the coolest months of the year, and this is when the ponds are drained and repaired. They are filled with wastewater in February. The plants are allowed to grow before the carp are introduced in March. More wastewater is added during the year. The carp are caught from May to December.

Industrial water

Industry uses a lot of water. Sometimes, cold water is used to cool equipment, or it may be used as part of the manufacturing process.

The warm wastewater from this power station in Hong Kong can be seen entering the sea.

Warm water problems

When water is used to cool equipment, it becomes warm, and then this warm water is often emptied back into a river or ocean. This may not seem bad, but, surprisingly, warm water can cause a lot of damage. Warm water holds less oxygen than cold water, so aquatic animals, especially fish, can die if the temperature of the water increases.

Water for manufacturing

Some industries, such as paper making and chemical manufacturing, use a lot of water. In some parts of the world, the wastewater is emptied into rivers and seas without any treatment. This causes water pollution. However, responsible manufacturers empty their wastewater into special lagoons where the pollutants can be removed and only clean water is allowed to drain out.

The color of the water has turned a rusty orange because wastewater from an industrial site is draining into this Australian stream.

Old mines

Old mines that are no longer in use can pollute rivers. Sometimes the underground passages trap water. The water picks up chemicals such as iron compounds from the surrounding rocks. This water may leak into rivers and cause pollution.

Did you know ...

Sometimes the warm water from power stations can be useful. The warm water can be sufficient to keep nearby water ice-free all winter. In Northern Canada, many birds are attracted to the ice-free lakes beside power stations because it allows them to feed all winter. In Australia and California, the warm water is used to create recreational lakes.

Farm water

The water that runs off fields in wet weather can harm the streams, rivers, and lakes into which it drains.

The water in this lake has turned green because there are millions of tiny algae floating in the water.

Fertilizers and algal blooms

Crop plants need a lot of nutrients, especially nitrates and phosphates, so farmers spray fertilizers containing the nutrients onto their crops. The nutrients are soluble, which means they dissolve in water. If heavy rain falls soon after the farmer has sprayed the fertilizer, the nutrients dissolve in rainwater. The rainwater may drain into local streams, rivers, and lakes, where the nutrients cause tiny plants called algae to grow more rapidly. Sometimes the algae form a layer, known as an algal bloom, over the surface of the water. When the algae die, they are broken down by microorganisms in the water. The microorganisms use up all the oxygen in the water, so fish and other aquatic organisms may die.

Silage

Another source of polluted water on a farm comes from silage. Silage is grass that is used to feed cattle in winter. Farmers make silage by cutting grass and storing it in a heap during the summer. It is covered by plastic to trap the heat. The grass sweats and water drains out of it. This water is full of nutrients and must not be allowed to drain into water courses; otherwise, it can cause an algal bloom.

It's my world!

Garden plants also need nutrients. You can buy fertilizers in liquid form or as pellets that can be sprinkled on the soil. A much better source of nutrients is a compost heap. Garden waste is put on a compost heap, where it is broken down. The resulting compost can be recycled onto the soil.

Food scraps from the kitchen can be placed on a compost heap where worms, fungi, and bacteria break down the food.

Creating wildlife habitats

In many towns and cities around the world, people are looking for more natural ways to treat sewage and other forms of wastewater.

Copying nature

Natural wetlands clean water by acting like a sponge. They soak up rainwater that runs off the land before it enters rivers and streams. As the water flows between the roots of the plants, the microorganisms around the roots break down the waste.

An artificial marsh can do the same. This is a combination of a sewage treatment plant and a reed bed. It can deal with large quantities of wastewater. Sewage is emptied into a tank and the solids settle out as sludge. The sludge is removed and broken down to make compost.

A woman walks along a path at Arcata Marsh, California. Not only does the marsh treat wastewater, but it is an important wildlife area.

Ponds and marshes

The wastewater from the tanks is piped into ponds, and microorganisms begin to break down the waste. Then the water is moved into a series of artificial marshes, where the mud around the roots of plants such as reeds and rushes is full of microorganisms and other decomposers. The water gets cleaner as it passes from one marsh to the next. The water that drains out of the last marsh is clean enough to be allowed into rivers or the sea.

Wildlife habitats

The artificial marshes create a wetland area that not only treats sewage but looks attractive and forms a wildlife habitat. The plants growing around the ponds and marshes attract various insects, birds, and mammals. Some artificial marshes have such a large number of bird species that they have been made into nature reserves.

Wastewater from a fish farm is emptied into plots where rice and other plants are grown. The plants use the nutrients in the water. Wildlife is common in and around this area.

Did you know . . .

More than 150 cities and towns in the United States have built artificial marshes to treat sewage. One successful marsh is Arcata Marsh in California. The marsh is home to so many different animals and plants that it has become an important wildlife reserve and attracts many tourists.

It's my world!

Many sewage treatment plants have wildlife areas. Look up your local sewage treatment plant on the Internet and see if they have any information about the animals and birds that can be found there. Those that have lots of birds often have an observation room where you can go to watch the birds.

Reusing and recycling water

Many people recycle aluminum cans, glass bottles, and newspapers, but wastewater can be recycled, too. Reusing and recycling water means that less fresh water needs to be used and less wastewater needs to be treated.

Using a rain barrel helps save water. You can also water plants during the cooler parts of the day to avoid water evaporation and pour water onto the soil slowly to help it soak in.

It's my world!

A lot of water runs off roofs, down drainpipes, and into the drains. Some of this water can be diverted into a rain barrel. Water collected in a rain barrel can be used to water the garden or wash the car. The larger the rain barrel, the greater the volume of water that can be saved.

Industrial recycling

Many industrial plants reuse water. For example, water that has been used to cool equipment can be stored on-site. Once it has cooled down, it can be used again.

Recycled water is also used in manufacturing processes such as paper making and dyeing carpets, and on construction sites where it may be used to mix concrete.

Many paper mills reuse water that is slightly dirty. This means they can reduce the amount of fresh water they use and have less dirty water to treat.

This golf course has been built on volcanic lava in Hawaii. The ground is dry, so large quantities of water have to be used to keep the grass alive. Wastewater could be used instead of clean water.

Did you know . . .

Toilets use lots of water. Each year, the average American uses 12,945 gallons (49,000 l) of water to flush about 166 gallons (630 l) of human waste down the toilet. In the United Kingdom (UK), the figure is lower at about 5,300 gallons (20,000 l) per year. By using the latest designs of toilet (which use just about a gallon of water per flush), this figure could be reduced to about 2,100 gallons (8,000 l).

Water for plants

There is no need to use drinking water to water golf courses, parks, and crops. Wastewater from sewage treatment plants can be used instead. There is an added benefit. The plants use the nutrients so the water is safe to drain into lakes and rivers. Recycling water in this way is important in desert areas where there is little rain.

The way ahead

There is not an unlimited amount of fresh water in the world. If people continue to use water at the current rate, there will be shortages as rivers and wells run dry, even in areas that normally have plenty of water.

This tourist development is in the Canary Islands where the climate is hot and dry for much of the year. Tourists use a lot of water, and that water has to be piped in from other areas during the busiest months.

Tourists and water

Often, new tourist resorts are built in places that receive very little water, for example, around the Mediterranean and in the deserts of Northern Africa. Tourists use a lot of water—they may shower several times a day and require clean towels and bed sheets. This means that the resort may use more than its fair share of water and leave people in the surrounding area without water. By being more careful about developments in the future, it may be possible to avoid water shortages.

Cutting down on waste

The best way to cut down on waste is to reduce the amount of water that we use. This could be as simple as cutting down on water that leaks out of pipes. It is estimated that as much as 40 percent of all of the water moved around some cities leaks into the ground. There are more losses from leaking pipes in homes and from faucets that are left running. We must think about how much water we are using every time we turn on a faucet. If we use less water, there will be less wastewater to treat.

It's my world!

There are many ways that you and your family could reduce the amount of water that you use in the home. If you have a water meter, take a reading and see how much you use in a week. Then try to reduce the volume of water you use. For example, don't let faucets drip, don't leave the water running while you brush your teeth, have a shower rather than a bath, and make sure the dishwasher is only used when it is full.

The level of water in this reservoir in the UK is at a record low at the end of a hot, dry summer. As more homes are built, there is an increasing demand for water, which may lead to water shortages.

Glossary

Bacteria
microscopic single-celled organisms;
some can cause disease

Biodegradable
able to be broken down naturally by
microorganisms such as bacteria and fungi

Compost
to break down garden waste; compost is a
soil-like material that is full of nutrients

Decomposition
the process by which something breaks
down

Decomposer
an organism such as fungi that causes
something to break down

Detergent
a type of soap used for cleaning clothes

Developed country
a country in which most people have
a high standard of living

Developing country
a country in which most people have a low
standard of living and poor access to goods
and services compared with people in a
developed country

Fertilizer
a substance that provides plants with
all the nutrients that they require

Lagoon
a large body of water

Pesticide
a chemical that is used to kill pests

Pollution
the release of harmful materials into
the environment

Recycle
to process and reuse materials in
order to make new items

Reduce
to lower the amount of waste that
is produced

Reuse
to use something again, either in the
same way or in a different way

Waste
anything that is thrown away,
abandoned, or released into the
environment in a way that could
harm the environment

Web sites

Ducks Unlimited

www.ducks.org/conservation/

Learn more about this leader in waterfowl and wetland conservation in North America.

Earth 911

www.earth911.org/master.asp

This Web site shows a variety of national and local U.S. recycling programs and events.

Save Water

www.savewater.com.au

Australian Web site looking at why we need to save water and how this can be done.

Water Recycling

www.waterrecycling.com/index.htm

Learn about alternative wastewater treatment at this site.

Water Recycling

www.waterrecycling.com/tableofc.htm

A U.S. Web site that looks at the ways water can be recycled and how waste water can be treated using artificial marshes.

World Wildlife Federation

www.panda.org/index.cfm

Web site of the WWF that looks at conservation around the world. There are sections on issues affecting fresh water and the oceans.

Index

DATE DUE
